T0064556

The Fates,
the Power,
and the
Great Joy

The Fates, the Power, and the Great Joy

Justin White

BALBOA.
PRESS

A DIVISION OF HAY HOUSE

Balboa Press books may be ordered through
booksellers or by contacting:

Balboa Press
A Division of Hay House
1663 Liberty Drive
Bloomington, IN 47403
www.balboapress.com
1 (877) 407-4847

Because of the dynamic nature of the Internet, any web addresses or
links contained in this book may have changed since publication and
may no longer be valid. The views expressed in this work are solely
those of the author and do not necessarily reflect the views of the
publisher, and the publisher hereby disclaims any responsibility for them.

The author of this book does not dispense medical advice or
prescribe the use of any technique as a form of treatment for physical,
emotional, or medical problems without the advice of a physician,
either directly or indirectly. The intent of the author is only to offer
information of a general nature to help you in your quest for emotional
and spiritual well-being. In the event you use any of the information
in this book for yourself, which is your constitutional right, the author
and the publisher assume no responsibility for your actions.

Any people depicted in stock imagery provided by Thinkstock are
models, and such images are being used for illustrative purposes only.
Certain stock imagery © Thinkstock.

Print information available on the last page.

ISBN: 978-1-5043-3362-7 (sc)
ISBN: 978-1-5043-3363-4 (e)

Balboa Press rev. date: 06/09/2015

The Fates

One man fell unto a desert. And there he wandered seeking freedom from the desolate land thrust upon him by the Fates. Very soon he found freedom, and his suffering was quickly forgotten for his joy. While this man's experience was not truly difficult, it did little for him; it did not possess the power to cause much reaction in him to grow, or look within himself to feel any depth of desire. And the totality of the man's soul looked upon the experience knowing it would be many more lives before he would be developed enough to experience anything of true depth. For the totality could see that the man had yet to seek beyond what was readily visible to his eyes, he had only a will for the surface of life, and he was preoccupied by a strong disrespect for others and an even deeper fear of life and death.

Another man was given the desert. And there he wandered seeking freedom from the harsh land. Suns rose and fell beyond his counting. The seasons turned and came full circle, and yet, freedom from the suffering of his days, and feet, and heart had not ended. And then, one day the scorching flat fell before him and fresh water trickled toward green life. His experience possessed far more power than the first man, and it achieved great feats for his entire being; far more than he or any other were aware.

Then another man fell to the desert, and even the Fates themselves held their breaths for what this man had agreed to undergo; for the Fates may only weave the threads given to them by free souls. And mortals are unaware of all that they freely choose as souls prior to incarnation, so they curse the Fates for their sufferings and their tragedies, though they have only themselves to, call it blame. The Fates know there is no blame; only choices made freely, from a state of strength, and great desire for fulfillment, for fun and adventure. What more, the Fates have long since radiated the vibrations of understanding that through great suffering the truest growth and beauty may be accomplished. Only through such limitation may our knowledge of limitlessness more fully evolve. Through experience of what may be opposite to our desires we come to more fully know our true desires, even by knowing we desire something completely opposite to our experience. And there are many ways to suffer for unfulfilled desires of all that would make us happy, but it will naturally lead to power and focus in the direction opposite all undesired experience. Every desire has a shadow, and every shadow has pure light as its source. The shadows of suffering are but phantoms and they will be turned away from, the view with our backs to the sun is beautiful, it adds perspective, but of course, our eyes may return to the source of light and absorb into that radiance. Until then the shadows are a matter of perspective, one that is perceived and experienced on many levels.

The man suffered many dark perspectives upon every level of being. Long cycles of experience revolved about for years, and the man became like an ancient thing: roaming, surviving, seeking, surrendering, fighting, crying, dying, living, laughing, and hoping for freedom from the desert. But in all that time the man became wise, strong to his core, understanding of others, and caring of himself. He suffered beyond limit. When he went beyond his limit and was suffering so completely he looked straight up into the sky and poured out a powerful call for something; for release from pain, for the deep and clear expression to existence of what he so desperately desired, for what he feared, and for a God if there was one. The man accepted death, the release of all that he was to all that is. He felt death within him, though his feet continued to walk, and his lungs continued to breathe in the air of life.

And finally, the path of destiny took the man to another hot day upon the desert of his life. His suffering had broken in some way. He had accomplished the levels of suffering he planned for himself in order to advance his own consciousness, and to alleviate some of the overwhelming suffering within the world beyond the desert. The man passed through complete fear to completely letting go. Though silence was all that could be heard in his ears, the depth of his call broke the heart of every spirit watching, and of the Fates weaving this horrible and wonderful destiny. So much so, that it was decided in their hearts that a rare gift be given to the man. And so, upon his path stood a spirit of divine wisdom disguised as a young girl.

And the girl said, "Please, take rest here where it is cooler, let your fears be forgotten for your dreams, I will sing you to sleep." Such a melody arose from the girl that instantly, the man became very tired and he lay down to sleep. As he slept he began to dream, and in his dreams he saw an enlightened being. So, he asked the being of light why he suffered so.

And the being said, "Because you sought to do amazing work for the evolution of your soul, and to help heal, along with many others, the negative energies within humanity, even the very planet that has taken in so much of their warring energies."

But he was not satisfied and felt sad and said, "I just don't see why anyone would choose all this."

And the enlightened being replied, "Your conscious being does not remember, but you are far more than you are currently aware. Before this life in the desert you were a soul of light. You looked upon this desert with clear knowledge that the opportunity to live here was one to be greatly prized. In this desert dreams fade, the light of life is blotted out by the shadow of death, and fear is faced head on. But for all its horror and dis-ease it provides the toughest training for the souls of the Universal Self to incarnate. It is in the desert that you wisely choose to live and suffer to a great extent, for great purpose, and for more than just yourself."

"But will it ever end?"

"It is not mine to say all of what will happen in your life here, but I may say with certainty that you planned for every possibility, and the big stuff that happens is primarily set in place by your own hand before your birth. You entered this world to forget all that you truly are, and all that this existence truly is; you came to not know, to not be happy, at least for some of your time, and to grow far stronger, far more developed than you were. The intensity of your experience offers to the evolution of the infinite mind of God something of invaluable worth. It offers to infinite unified energy a far more powerful knowledge, experience, and/or activation and potentiation of Its Self. But my brother, your life will change, and you are destined for such fulfillment. I could not promise you that your life would be full of happiness even if it were to be so; but no matter what, I can promise you that whatever occurs is the perfect path for you in your journey to achieving absolute fulfillment."

And the man awoke to the night sky so full of bright stars. He awoke with the memory of his dream fairly clear upon his mind, and for a while he just laid there in wonder and enjoyment of the warm feelings that came over him. And then, he began to walk, his eyes fixed upon the night sky. Hope had returned to him, and he walked, and he watched the night sky with nervous desire for an angel, or some manner of miracle to come to him, only hardly believing that something might happen. As he walked through the night his mind was alive with hope and faith; with thoughts of strength and acceptance of whatever comes because he at least would always have himself to offer Love and acceptance, he would Love the earth and sky, his bright day star a radiant beauty, and the night satellite his baby boy. So long as he lived it would serve great purpose for his self, and for all others. His mind was locked on the nuances held within this vision, these strange and comforting ideas. But still, his pain persisted and as his feet would stand upon what was the distant desert horizon, his eyes saw only another horizon and another view of endless desert in between.

The man believed in his experience and amidst the dark desert he came to truly believe in the light, in life, in beauty, meaning, and in his own power despite his seemingly powerless position. And upon the desert earth he sat in meditation; his eyes closed and his breath became calm and deep, and his mind settled deep within his being. And within those depths a vision was perceived. He saw the lives of his soul all in a line. There were thousands of holographic manifestations of beings strung out before him, and each one possessed valuable aspects for the whole. He saw his soul incarnate as a beautiful person, as an ugly one, as rich, as poor, fat, tall, short, skinny, smart, stupid, as spiritual, as not, and in other lives he saw beings that were beyond his understanding; they were highly advanced in total development, and he saw the power his suffering contributed, he saw the stream of lives back away into the distance to reveal a circle, a complete union of vast experience. The circle itself then began to spin with greater and greater speed until one life was left for him to see emerging from the brilliant spectacle like a pulsar.

In an instant he stood upon what seemed heavenly ground and the one life was coming toward him. The man was in awe because the being was radiant with bright colors of light, and with the brightest white, and colors he had never seen, and his feet did not touch the ground, instead he hovered above it. The two came face to face and the being smiled upon the man and said, "I am you,

you are me, and we are complete, I offer you all the Love, wisdom, and power of our total experience." And just like that, the being turned away and began to rise into the air, into a white star in the sky, into the pure Love that is the source of all, but before the light enveloped him, the being turned back and a light shot out of him into the man. And the man opened his eyes. He was in the desert.

The man stood up and began to walk as he always had, but he was changed forever. No matter what, or how long he would suffer, he knew that he deeply believed in something so much more. He believed that all was as it should be, and in the beauty and perfection of the path he was on, no matter where that path would lead him. He knew that if he suffered it was for great purpose, for his soul and for the soul of all others, and if all could be seen there would be nothing any of us would choose to change; for when all is seen one's heart is overcome by the absolution of the beauty of Love.

He believed in his and all others' intrinsic worth and honorability. He believed that no matter what he need not feel guilt or shame in himself, and that he was always deserving of his own self Love, acceptance, and respect. And then, as he walked with joy and Love bubbling up from within he saw the desert fall away and cool waters flowing before him like only in his dreams. He could hardly believe his eyes, emotions and utter joy flowed from the man and took him into the sacred waters. And in those waters awaited a girl of such beauty that the man's breath was lost, his heart beat in excitement, and his life was complete. And the Fates smiled with joy upon the man and all that his soul had freely chosen to experience, for they could see every thread of every life for every single soul in every world within every universe, and they weaved its perfect pattern with wonder.

Wow to the Living

Woe to the living!

Not because they will soon be dead

Or rather that they would enter life beyond

Woe to them that they are alive

For in life they are dead to all the life and the light

The light that those who have died go back to

The light that they are completely saturated by

And yet the living cry

When people die

Though they are the ones who become truly alive

Woe to the living!

They can't see a thing

In life it is too dark

So they fear anything near and kill and build an ark

To float upon all the blood they spill

THE FATES, THE POWER, AND THE GREAT JOY

In God's name

Or in the name of justice, or democracy, it's all the same

There are no evildoers

There are only dishonest, disrespectful, and selfish rulers

Woe to the living!

Woe to them because they do not know

All the beauty and purpose of woes

Their eyes are not privy to how it all goes

There will be highs and lows

But the river flows

Just let the sand squeeze between your toes

And stand, even full of fear

But face into the wind

Believing that there is something here

That may calm every fear

And you may say it with a smile

Woe to the living!

Because you believe and you perceive

Absolute beauty

Meaning and power in this great adventure

And your woes will become wows

Deep experiences to open your heart to

Looking up into the sky so blue

Wow to the living!

That is Crazy

We may naturally think that certain beliefs and ideas are crazy and that others are not, but anything sounds pretty crazy to me. If there is a God, that is crazy man. If there isn't one, that is crazy too. If Jesus ever walked this earth and was divine, or an enlightened being, that is crazy. If the Buddha experienced nirvana, if Muhammad was God's Prophet, if any founder of any religion was ever anything cool, then that is crazy. If there are countless other worlds full of life upon levels that are comparable to our own, as well as, what we might understand to be metaphysical beings, or those of a higher evolutionary development in terms of their physical, mental, and emotional being, then that is crazy. If there is absolutely no meaning to our universe and humans have occurred simply by chance, that is crazy. If there were no existence, that would be crazy. The fact that there is anything is crazy. Any idea, any reality is crazy really.

There are so many different beliefs and ideas out there. I think there is plenty of basis in reality for most of them, even if so much is distorted from the truth. It's about how clearly that truth is seen, but in this life it will inevitably be very blurry at times. I can understand any belief, any idea, any perspective, even if it is a crazy one. Naturally, our minds are capable of being quite distorted, imbalanced, or underdeveloped, but each mind also possesses the potential for the opposite of all that. But even a clear mind will think and express ideas that sound crazy, no matter what they say. If there is a single Truth that could be told to explain all things it would sound crazy, even if it were absolutely true. If there is a unified field theory it is crazy stuff.

What about dinosaurs? Them things were crazy big lizards that walked this very earth, and for many more years than human feet have, and in all likelihood ever will. If we were never told about them, and someone said today that such creatures once existed on this planet we would think it was crazy. Beaches, blizzards, the sun, the moon, happiness, sadness, death, and making Love upon this spinning sphere of matter thrust from our star billions of years ago; it's all one unbelievable experience. You may see and experience horrible things, but all things can be healed and this crazy blur of a ride can rise to a high place with a clear view. It is a view full of beauty. That view lies within the sovereignty of your own mind, within your own efforts to seek, to desire, and to find within yourself. But, of course, you may think all that is crazy.

Not an Expert

I am not an expert in any field, be it spirituality, physics, astronomy, physiology, history, grammar, or anything else. I make no claim to be free from error, or from possessing disparate thoughts that may apparently conflict. There is so much that is unclear to me, and of the things I know, I know that so much may be mistaken. I do not claim to originate any idea, any potential message, or any understanding of anything whatsoever. I have my teachers, my healers, and my sources of inspiration and study that pass through my own individual discrimination and will to seek. I think for myself, I misunderstand plenty, and I learn from my teachers. I believe what I believe, I think what I think, and any of it could change at any moment. Any of it could be wrong, any of it could be right. It is for each individual to use their own powerful freedom of thought and will to choose what they think, and how they want to react to and treat all things. So if you read all of what follows, know that it is self-expression; it is opinion, and art, and whatever it is to you.

Every Sound We Make

God is every sound we make

Every heart at the moment it will break

Every childish soul who only knows how to take

And everything in life that does not
seem to be for goodness sake

God is in everything man thinks is so wrong

THE FATES, THE POWER, AND THE GREAT JOY

And for everyone who has been deeply hurting for so long

There is a divine plan for you

And every ounce of your pain is healing
you even though it hurts you too

Souls who do not truly grow, develop, and discover

The path leading to their deepest
dreams; they do not truly suffer

So the deeper you suffer know that this is how you uncover

Everything blocking your eyes and your heart

And your life is such a more beautiful work of art

Than it is for those who do not truly
suffer, truly Love, and truly dream

Suffering, tragedy, pain, heartbreak, death;
these things are not what they seem

They are all players on God's team

And they never lose

Even though they will make you feel
lost and unable to choose

Anything you really want to win

Have faith, you have no idea the beauty
and perfection you're in

In Times of Pain and Suffering

In times of pain and suffering turn to nature, look to the sky, look to the trees and the flowers…take time and look at them, go near to them and they will help reconcile the forces in you that are painful to you. They will help you more than you know; they are alive, they see you, they feel you, and they reach out to you at all times to reveal to you the hidden truths and beauties that have been lost to you and that you may find in their silence, in their presence, in their simplicity, majesty, and hidden harmony.

In times of pain and suffering go to where children are, to where they play, and let their playfulness surround you and remind you…let them remind you of something that can never truly die in you; it may only be lost and forgotten for a time. It is their connection to the heart of life that you may remember through their example; and the heart of life is the desire to expand, to play, and laugh, and Love as much as possible. When you are ready go out and play. Go out and exercise so that you can remember that your heart is not just for Love and joy; it is for the will in you that is infinitely free and has the ability to utilize every painful experience.

You are all the masters of yourselves, and all that you have ever known about yourself and all that is may truly transform and become more like what you have dreamed. Play and fight, laugh and cry. You don't need to wonder why and wish to die. Your life is not a lie, nor your dreams that heaven and earth seem to deny; it is just that you are in the middle of a great journey leading to the fulfillment of those dreams, and of dreams you have yet dare to dream because they are so beautiful. And when those dreams finally do come true they will fill your heart with deep abundance; if you had never lost hope for such dreams it would not be so, not with the perfection that you are all destined for.

In times of pain and suffering watch comedies, watch "America's Funniest Home Videos", and seek out all that may bring you laughter. In times of pain and suffering don't forget to breathe. Your breath is more important than you think. Center your breathing in your powerful solar plexus and bring it all the way up into your heart, all the way to the top of your chest. Let go of whatever person, idea, desire, or reality that you think is necessary for you to be happy. Nothing is necessary except your own breath and the beating of your heart. Love them, but let them go too. Life will still be able to bring you people and realities that will fill your life with joy and thankfulness. But things take time. They take time, effort, and at times effortlessness. But never doubt that the continued living of your life is worth the effort. You and your life are worth every effort, and when it gets effortlessly happy; what can I say, I desire this for you dearly because it is there. It is free for all to find.

Listen to music, sing out loud, dance around to free up your lifeless body, and bring yourself back to life. Run. Put away the gun, whether it is a real one in your hand, or a metaphorical one in the form of all your negative beliefs and mental attitudes towards yourself, your life, and all things. Write, talk to kind people, don't talk about your problems, read inspiring quotes, jump up and down, turn that frown upside down, and go punch a clown. Don't wear the color brown, wear white and bright colors, clean your room and your body, and wash away the past, it need not last, every second is going by so fast and so slow... you don't need to act like a ho, and drugs and alcohol will not stop you from feeling so low. You've got to find a way to believe in this as meaningful, not a mistake, and learn to go with a deeper flow that has learned there is a big part of us that must let go of all control. Care about yourself, feel Love and compassion for this mind, body, and soul. Pray to life, pray to God, pray to the angels, pray to Limitless Light, pray to the spirit of beauty, peace, and Love...pray for help and know that you are helped when you ask for help; whatever you open yourself up to will come to you; I pray that what comes is a revolution within your own mind such that you know your power and your worth.

If you open yourself up to anger, judgment, war, hate, and the rejection of circumstance by freely choosing to believe those things are necessary for you, by focusing on them, by maintaining those mental and emotional attitudes, then those energies will come to you. But if you pray to all those good things and fight for every beautiful and peaceful attitude then those energies will begin to gravitate to you. But you must take the time to build up the right mass and momentum so that the right things will come your way by the gravity of your focus; by your prayers and positive efforts, by your Love and peace, by your belief in your ability to fulfill every desire and every dream. Good things and bad things come according to their own intelligent rhythm, they may last however long they last, but things are always moving and changing; enjoying more of the good requires moving along with this rhythm that is the natural flow of your life. I believe there is great meaning to all life, and that the experiences in each life have meaning and purpose for the greater development of your soul. Pray and one day you may look back on this from a state of true bliss. Everything good can happen for you, it can all happen for you, every dream sweetheart.

Blood and Guts

Blood and guts...You can suffer for years and give up a thousand times, and rise to fight after every collapse, only to fall again, and again. It is not a matter of never giving up; it's about getting up after you give up. Get up to fight for yourself, always. The fighter is an important aspect of who we all are. We can survive, and we can thrive. Suffering will make you weak, that is perfectly acceptable, it is a part of the training for the fighter; to know great fear and weakness deepens one's knowledge and experience of true faith and strength. There is bravery and an animalistic ferocity to the human heart and soul, to the quest of a spiritual seeker.

You've got to want it, no guts no glory. You got to take all of your fear and doubt and shove it all up life's ass. Where is the fighter? Where is the focus? Where is the effort? Believe in yourself. Give it everything you've got.

Let every fear and pain and doubt feed your hunger. You will fear, you will doubt…accept it and let it all go, and go. You can suffer, and lose, and learn to fear until that is all that makes sense to you. And then, you can win, you can be happy; you can change, and grow, and go to places in yourself that are incredible.

A Blink of an Eye

God…What do you really think that is like, God that is? Do you really think it's some guy up in the sky? I wish you could look through my eyes at this moment, because I am just a man, and yet, I have felt things that move deeper than what can be said in words. I am just a man. God is unspeakable. It refers to an energy that is so unbelievably powerful It forms the infinite universes of light and life in the blink of an eye. Every photon that has ever been given oscillation within the expanding movement of space, every atom that has been displaced from the perfect unity of space and time with its rotational velocity, every star that has ever formed due to the aggregation of those particles, or energy fields, and every galaxy that has ever spun its way throughout the evolution of but a single universe, is but a blink of an eye upon the face of Infinity.

I look up at the stars and I think, "God…what are you? What is it to understand that being, that energy, that essence, that infinitely amazing thing that is and forms all things?" And a flash enters my mind, like a simple picture of light in motion. And as I recall the flash of an image that just came to me it is as if there were a smile in the midst of that light, and innumerable flowers blossoming and falling from a skyless vision. There is a beauty that can never be described. There is pure Love. God is one power of a Love that is infinitely intelligent, infinitely alive, infinitely happy, and infinitely meaningful. And that is what we are all a part of, that is our truest identity.

We may feel that there are so many mistakes and horrible things in life, but it could all be over in the blink of an eye. Such a thought is aimed upon releasing the baggage and freeing the heart and mind to welcome life. We exist. We are here...my God; every good thing and every bad thing falls away equally in the face of complete extinction, and there the pure foundation is felt under foot. That foundation is the pure wonder at existence; at the mysterious miracle it is to be alive. In the blink of an eye it will all be gone, it could end at any moment, and it could change for the great better just as quickly.

I Am

I am alive

I am good

I am free

I am in the right place for me

I am the creator of my own reality

I am Light

I am Love

I am amazingly beautiful inside

I am one with God

All others are too

All is the pure perfect

Energy of Infinity

I am Loved

I am worthy of respect

All others are Loved

And worthy of equal respect

All are equal to the highest worth

All are Infinite

Infinite life

Infinite joy

Infinite beauty

Infinite desire

Infinite power

Infinite Love

Infinite intelligence

Intelligent Infinity

Infinity within everyone

Surrounded we are

By limitless light

Broken Down

Once you are completely broken down you can find what you truly believe in. When all is lost for you, or when you truly suffer you may deal with things from a powerful perspective. It is a powerful experience that possesses an exciting potential for change, deepening of strength, realization of truth, growth, and the opening of your heart. When for whatever reasons, there is no proof of anything for you, and you don't know what to think or do your mind would go to deep questions like, "What is all this life about? What is the reason for this suffering? Is there any reason to anything? Why am I here? Is there truly a God? What happens when we die?" No matter what your ideas about those questions may be, the suffering provides you with a powerful and mysterious opportunity. It is powerful to feel such emotions, such fear, and pain, and confusion. There is power in the experience, as well as in its potential to fuel great things within you; things that are deep within and would not be unearthed were it not for suffering.

But we can throw all those questions out, and any possible answers; what then are we left with, but an existence in which there is the potential for highs and lows? Do things happen for a reason or not? Is there

Love or not? Is it all just chemicals, carbon compounds, blood and bones, for one birth and for one death, and then nothing else? There are multiple planets around our sun, which is one star among about 250 billion stars in a single galaxy. There are billions upon billions of galaxies in this universe, and it is all for these beings that we are, and it is only physical-chemically driven life? I don't know man; I think there is a lot more going on. The mere scale, majesty, and order of the physical universe beg the suspicion of so much more.

But let's go ahead and throw all that out. Let's say there is no meaning and no God. There is still an unbelievable universe of energy. That is what all things in the physical universe are, is energy. Gravity exists and it leads to groupings of energy to form all that we know, all that we as a planet are, and all the billions of galaxies and stars. What an amazing thing. People exist. How amazing. But why and how remain a complete mystery. Because the question will necessarily lead to asking why there is space or time. Why is there any energy, gravity, space, or time? These manifestations are what lead to the formation of everything in our physical understanding. So why? How did these things come to be at all? Why anything at all? If there is not even some manner of physical or energetic source to all that is then was there ever nothing? There was either always something, or at some time there was nothing. Whether we come from nothing, or from something, all things share the same origin, from a single evolutionary stream. It may possess meaning, or it may not. It may be any shade of grey.

You are the one that must decide at the toughest turns what it is to you. You are faced with coming up with your own answers, and changing them however you see fit. If there is no meaning in the evolution of energy within the physical universe then it is still beautiful to me. There is beauty out there amidst the infinite explosions of stellar light and galactic spirals. It may feel a dark and dirty place, but when you see a picture of this planet it looks bright and innocent as it completes its revolutions around our sun. It is a creature of natural order and of its own individual movement; a movement that harmonizes with all other bodies within its system. It may all be worthless and ugly to you, but you at least have the power of mind to conceive it as such, and the free individuality to maintain your views despite anyone else's view. It is beautiful and remarkable for that to exist in my opinion. It is beautiful and miraculous for there to be even a single world in this universe; for there to be the opportunity to live a life, however horrible and meaningless you may perceive that life to be, to have pets, to laugh, to have fun, to have sex, and children, and your own self to develop and desire what you may.

At the ends of yourself you are faced with fear of the unknown, with fear of pain and death, with fear of loss of all that you desire; within yourself the choice may be made to face that moment with a kind of stupid bravery, and a letting go to Love whatever may come. But why? Either you believe there is meaning, or you don't. Either one is understandable, and will have a significant effect upon the world you create with your mind. Surely, you will have fear, and you will meet challenges of your days without Love, without belief that there is good meaning behind what has happened, but that does not mean such is the case.

Feeling that way, and experiencing suffering in general may be likened to lifting weights. Without a weight in your hand you can easily lift your hand to your shoulder, but with a heavy weight the same movement becomes difficult, it causes pain, fatigue, and a breaking down of muscle tissue. However, that very resistance, that pain is what causes the muscles to develop more strength. So, does your suffering make you the victim of the weight of life, or of your own stupidity, or of another's machinations? Or is it a meaningful process within your own self-development? All the suffering and mysteries of life are yours to work with. There is limitless potential for ways to understand things, to react to situations in life, and to treat yourself and others. And within those potentials lies power and freedom. It is the power of your thoughts; your thoughts affect you and others far more than most believe, at least in my mind. Your thoughts are energy, and that energy may be freely wielded in whatever ways you will.

I might only suggest the persistent attempt and desire to treat yourself and others with as much understanding and respect as possible. It certainly doesn't seem to be a thing that would lead you to less happiness when all is said and done. I think that when others treat us without respect and acceptance it is more an issue within their own self, as well as possible clues to our own imbalances. Others have hidden pains and blockages of energy that hinder completely smooth relationships. Likewise, our issues are primarily within our own self, our own fears, pains, and blockages lead us into discordance first with our self, and then with others. You can persist with whatever you want. You may be a real tough dude, or a pretty girl, or a rich man, or a respected community figure; but are the thoughts in your mind leading you toward peace or war, toward Love and faith or hate and fear, toward victimhood or enlightenment, toward just satisfying your own worldly desires, or giving energy and support to all that you see?

So What

Everything about every religion could be a farce. There could have been no Jesus, no Buddha, no miracles, or enlightened masters in any respect. We could analyze the Bible and every religious work and uncover all that is a lie, all that is mistaken about our understandings of who wrote it and why; to reveal that there was never any divine inspiration, and yet this would not prove that there is no God. Every religion could be a complete lie, and it would mean nothing. I am not saying that religions are lies and these people did not exist, perhaps they did not exist and live the precise lives that most of us imagine; I am saying that it is of no true consequence. My beliefs in our totality and in meaning to existence do not rest on the details of any man's life, nor in the historical accuracies and purity of intentions within the creators of our religious books. No one needs to think like me, and I don't even think that it is in everyone's best interest to think like me. We must all think like we do, but if your free thoughts would naturally lead your mind to similar thoughts as my opinions, or if mine seem to offer something you think might be true, then so be it. And if you think completely opposite to me then so be it.

To my knowledge, there is a great deal about religion, our religious founders, and historical fact that is quite mistaken. But even if it were all bullshit my response would be, "So what?" It would not mean that there isn't a God, or meaning to life, or spiritual things to experience. In my opinion, so much of what we generally understand to be historical, scientific, and religious/spiritual fact is quite mistaken; it does not very accurately correlate with a clear vision of reality. That is not to say it is all wrong, or even mostly wrong; however, an understanding may be substantially mistaken without being mostly wrong. We may see things much more clearly, much more beautifully, respectfully, and calmly. There are many subtleties to put in order, and fuzzy understandings to bring in focus. It is not even necessary for us to do so though, all I am saying is that the potential is there, and that no matter what any of us find there is no reason, no reality, no scientific, or historical fact that need sway you from feeling safe to believe that there is more to life than meets the eye.

The Goal

Everything is a part of my quest, my goal. Physical exercise, stretching, lifting weights, meditation, yoga, and nutrition are all about energy. I want to look good, and thus feel good about myself, and that is a part of the energy, but it is far from all of it. I seek the highest and most developed state in my evolution as a mind/body/ spirit, as a soul manifesting in this manner of being. There are many physical activities that may promote the rising of energy within. But of course, it is all intimately connected with mental and spiritual faculties as well. All is a part of the quest, all is connected. But there is so much more. These ideas basically convey the essences of power and wisdom, or the seeking for power and balance within the systems of energy that we are. Yet, there is Love. Love and peace in my heart, a beautiful relationship, and sexy sex serve the quest; the development and expression of our natural energy. But there is so much more because to look in a girl's eyes and to be completely overcome by attraction: physically, sexually, emotionally, mentally, and spiritually is to experience something that is beyond power and wisdom. It is beyond any goal. It needs not any purpose to fulfill the reason why; the power and the beauty are undeniable and uncontainable. The goal throughout all is a state of being within the self that is, suffice to say, balanced and enlightened.

All We Have Wrought

There is fear in you, there is anger, and hate

And late, and a horrible mate

You aren't doomed to meet a terrible fate

This is not karma

You might as well forget the dharma

Because you are all here

The end is not near

I can understand every reason to fear

And doubt any real meaning or design

But there is something in me that won't resign

To no more than physicality

Or meaningless atrocity

And I can't really say why

There are many reasons to reply

But it goes beyond that

Unto the depths of mystery I must tip my hat

When life has shown me great pain

And all is lost I would fain

Believe that there is a consciousness that hears me

A purpose to all that we can see

But all of existence is miraculous whether or not

There is any purpose to all we have wrought

Intelligence

Sometimes I feel that what passes for real intelligence is cynicism and a thoroughly negative view of the world, and of life. Forgive me, I don't mean to say that anyone expressing these sorts of things is precisely and necessarily unintelligent, but I certainly think that so much of what is going on in this world, and in this existence remains to be seen and felt by them. You may use your mind to communicate well thought out and articulated arguments with many facts to back you up, but what you are really saying is that you don't truly believe in life, in humanity, in purpose to anything, or in your own self. To so many of you out there life seems like such a horribly fucked up thing. Yes, you do see some positivity and some purpose too, but it is such a weak little consolation in comparison to all that you see as wrong, unwise, unjust, unsalvageable, and unmistakably tragic.

I have a lot of things I could say to contend with such views, but even if I could argue everything perfectly the point cannot be to prove anything to anyone. Everyone is free to think as they will, and there is no real proof to be offered. One may know many things to back up their own point of view, and if they are intelligent enough they might convince you of their argument, even if it is a rather stupid one, but the fact remains that there is no real proof. There is no proof that life is meaningless, or that it is meaningful. There is no undeniable proof thus far that atoms consist in such a way as physicists have imagined, or that the distant galaxies in relation to our own are receding due to the "Big Bang", or that mass and gravity truly curve a mere four dimensional space-time as Einstein conceived of it; nor is there undeniable proof that God exists, or that someone is truly in Love with you, or that you are in Love with them, or that there is anything after we die, or that there isn't. There is no proof that you can't be truly in Love, that there absolutely isn't a God, or angels, or great meaning to every little horrible and wonderful thing that has ever occurred upon this planet. There is no proof that there aren't billions upon billions of other worlds out there that are full of intelligent and peaceful life. No one person is exactly like you, and not all life must necessarily be like humanity.

I offer nothing that is truly intelligent, or original, or provable, but I profess that I believe in life. I believe in the beauty of this vast existence that we are a part of, and I believe that it all occurs with good reason, with powerful purpose; and that wisdom, justice, and Love reign over all that is viewed as bad and horrible in this world. I don't think it is so intelligent to have such a poor and depleted view of everything, of human tragedies; because you are really saying that you don't believe in it completely, in life, in the purpose of difficulty, pain, and heartbreak. I have had great difficulty, pain, and heartbreak and I truly and deeply believe in them with everything that I am. True intelligence to me can never be found in big words and negative views of life, nor in quantity of information held within the brain as opposed to quality; intelligence to me will always find symmetry, it will perceive rhythm, and order, and beauty. A less intelligent perception will see disorder, chaos, asymmetry, and ugliness because it simply does not yet see the whole picture with much clarity, thus its view is an incomplete and distorted one, and that's how it makes you feel, incomplete in your- self and distorted from harmony with all that is.

Toward Annihilation

There are all these spiritual and mental/emotional things I wish for humanity, but money is an important issue in order to survive in our society. A true and fair distribution of wealth would sound an effective solution. This does not mean taking from the rich, though it would include the end of the salaries taken by the upper echelons of big business, and every ridiculous profit made from truly unethical practices; it could primarily mean limiting the government's paycheck. If we took away all the money we spent on protecting ourselves and ensuring that we can kill everyone else what a fortune that would be! Or maybe we could just print our own money instead of paying interest to central banks, but all of that is just symptomatic of mental/emotional dis-ease within the minds of the masses. We share responsibility for all that is in this world, and we have the ability to transform it into a world and a way of life you wouldn't dare dream or feel worthy of today.

But in order to do all that there needs to be real peace in the world. And in order to have that level of peace in the world we must find peace within ourselves. Accepting the self for all its imperfection and for all its perfection cannot be fully divorced from achieving peace between nations. Everything is connected, and your relationship with yourself is done unto the whole of existence; it is done to everyone, to everything, to the one you Love the most, and it may aid the world in achieving peace. It and you may be a part of ending a recurring theme in humanity's history, that is, the few attempting to control and manipulate the many and reserving most of the resources for themselves; all the while instilling fear in the masses and leading them toward annihilation, or at least collapse of the empire, or what have you.

O God

O God, by the sum of every pain that could ever be, and surely is in my soul, release me from these flames. These are more than words, this is living, and it is dying; for I am a dead man. The cries of my torture all these years have rung throughout eternity and put fear in your angels. And every soul that ever was hears in their heart the deafening shrieks of my torment. And in that silent roar of resounding noise they feel within them all they might ever fear to lose, to suffer, the sum of all that may be suffered.

O God let what I have dreamed finally come to be, for I am no more. I am completely surrendered, given up, and forgotten unto my own self. What past was mine is flung from all memory, even what hope could be; it is gone, as am I, as well every fear, and every moment; every whisper of a thing rises from where it may make birth in a man, in me, and gently floats away without any effort to hold on to life. All things rise up from me, my eyes cease to even watch the chance for my hands to grab hold of what dreams they might contain, they begin to close and die and forget why.

O God, I can hold on no longer, or at least, I no longer wish to do so. No more...no more. My hands are open, my heart and soul welcome the dark release of death as if it were a beloved star of light and Love. Let me be free, for even though I can see reasons for all that is, my will turns to not any longer be...living and dying the same way I have for far too long. How long ago did I first fall to my knees, how many times since, and how long has it been since then? I want this no more. This cycle must end; one way or another.

The Light

I am standing still in the rain

It doesn't matter how much there is pain

The more I am destroyed

The more is created in me

It is a mystery

But there is something that is completely free

There is a deep power

It reveals a fascinating hour

Out of a season so cold and dry

And the confusion of why

But there is always a sky

You do not know

All the stillness and the power so

Take a step back and find it in you

The reason for all that we go through

It will stop you

It will revolutionize you

It will make your heart anew

Like Love and happiness were things you never knew

Not until your world was shattered

And you found out what really mattered

Time must move as it does

And change things from how it was

No matter how slow

Things go

I hope you know

When it is all over

You will be happy

And strong

Your life wasn't wrong

Everyone and everything will be alright

You will walk into the Light

And you are the Light

Logic

You may think it goes against all logic that there is a God, or spirituality, or metaphysicality, but shouldn't it also go against logic for anything to exist at all? Why should there be a universe, any energy, light, space, or time? Forget people and this planet, why and how does anything else at all exist? It should go against all logic for a single photon to exist. The more logical minds would point out all that is illogical about things such as faith and believing in God, never realizing that their own perspective must first take for granted a similarly unbelievable premise; it may be argued that it is just as illogical for there to be a God (or consciousness connecting all things) as it is for the universe to exist at all. Even if we understood so much more than we do now in purely logical scientific terms as far as how the universe began, how it functions, precisely of what it is composed and so forth, we would inevitably come to the question of why.

If there is no reason why, which in all logic should be the case, "how" remains the baffler of said logic. Let us presume that the photon was the first thing to come into physical manifestation. Well how did it do so? Let us say that it was due to some sort of potential interaction, some movement within or between space and time that resulted in such a particle of electromagnetic radiation. Okay, well how did space and time come into being? How is just as baffling to logic as why if you go back far enough to the most basic questions. How did particles of any nature, of any substance or mass ever logically come to exist within a spatial and temporal system? There must be some cause, some primal interaction or motion at the most basic level. I think logic and science can explain this, but not without taking a leap of faith, not without going beyond the same sort of strictures religions have put up and endeavors such as our sciences might have once hoped to free us from.

At some point, for some reason or for none, the universe, constituted at least by space and time, began to expand outward in every direction. This must have a cause, without a cause it would not be. The mystery is maddening, intriguing, exciting, and fucking crazy. What is more basic than space and time? What came before these things? And how did it come to be? How can there be any true logic in this completely illogical existence we find ourselves in, when it is illogical for anything to exist at all? The universe operates according to its own natural laws, its own logic, but how did this logical law abiding system come to be formed, and by what elements? By what elements more basic than those found in the periodic table? If everything can be logically explained then logically explain the beginning of everything.

At this point in our understanding we may at least move to concede the fact that logic must presume something illogical. It must presume that the universe began to expand by some unknown cause, and that there was a universe to expand in the first place. How was there a universe to be expanded? This is the illogical presumption; it must be accepted as a given that there was a universe, or at least the seeds of that universe to then evolve into what we perceive today. It is illogical because after all is deduced and ordered we come to a beginning that must be conceded for logic to begin to order and deduce therefrom; because if we deduce all to nothing in the beginning, how can we logically explain producing our universe out of that genesis, out of nothing? And it seems logical to me that cosmology should deduce to nothing in the beginning; because this came from that, and that from this, and this before that until there was nothing in the beginning, or else you must propose there was always something, which does not sit well with logic. If there was always this universe of something how is that possible? How does it exist if it always was? And in our universe there is constant motion, change, and evolution, this does not lend itself to the nature of something always existing. Logic can only begin with something and work from there. So logic needs a miracle, it needs something illogical in order to begin, to have something to order and make expansions upon, which it may later deduce therefrom.

Any genesis is illogical; if all began out of nothing, then how did it begin? If all always was, or if something always was for that matter, how? If Conscious Infinity, the Creator, or God chose to begin such a universe then that is illogical as well. No matter what we must concede the illogical to begin to be logical. Unless you think it is logical for there to be nothing, and then, for there to be something, somehow, without the conscious will of an intelligence; and for that nothingness to produce, out of no intelligent design, without cause, and for no reason, a universe of spectacular order upon so many levels, and all the intricacies, subtleties, nuances, and life! Life out of nothing...anything from nothing is a miracle, it is magical, it is completely illogical!

Meditation

It has been the single most important practice in my life for spiritual development. Most of the time there is no profound experience. It seems very mundane, even a complete failure. There are many thoughts in our brains, it is difficult to relax, to be comfortable, awake, and focused. If you practice meditation it will benefit you enormously even if you don't know it. Just keep at it, daily, even for one minute each night, or morning, or whenever. All you need is breathing meditation. Just sit down in a chair with your bare feet on the ground and focus on your breathing. You may sit on the ground cross legged of course, but be comfortable, and sit up straight. Breathe in deeply, expand the rib cage and bring the breath up high into the chest so that your lungs fill with air. Breathe in through your nose and out through your mouth making an "S" sound, or very little sound. The "S" sound gives you more to focus on. Your thoughts will wander that is fine. Practice realizing that your thoughts have wandered and bring your attention back to your breathing. Say to yourself, "Back to my breathing…all that exists is my breathing…all that exists is my breathing." And breathe. Thoughts will wander again and again. Do it again and again. Just relax and know that there is no way to fail or meditate wrong. It is more about finding even a moment of calm, and the persistence of one's will to do something like meditation, as well as the faith that something so simple could possibly be of any meaningful resource to you. It is seeking within the self, and within the self lies infinity itself.

I Am Thankful

Thank you for this day and praise be to the miracle of existence. Give us this day our daily bread and all the vital energy that we may sustain with harmony. God, you are all that there is; the unity of all energy, infinite and endless. Upon this day we ask of you to lead us not into disharmony within ourselves, or between one another, but deliver us from imbalanced manifestations of energy. Though we accept and honor every misqualified expression of energy and every despairing reality; for they are purposeful portions of a grander experience, which when understood in a larger context constitute perfect catalyst for evolution, understanding, and Love; we yet ever seek to experience a state of being that is in greater harmony with You.

We seek the truth, we seek balance within, we seek fulfillment in every way for every reason. We seek thusly for individual well-being, for mutual well-being, and for the well-being of the divine.

Today I call upon my Higher Self and the pure Love of God to give to me all that they, as one unitary principle, or essence, feel is the highest and best for me in this moment. And I ask of them to help me to balance my lower energies so that as much of God's sacred energy will flow up into my heart as possible. Let it bless me, my life, and all others with the beautiful gift of its grace. It is all for Love. I seek to Love and to be Loved, and Loved by myself most of all. Please help me to accomplish all this, and thank you, I am thankful for all things, for there being any life at all, and for all that my life has been, there is meaning and beauty in it all.

Somewhere Serene

I want to learn a thousand different things

I want to do a thousand different things

I want to jump in every direction

I want to experience so many beautiful connections

I want to shout and sing

I want to live and dream and eat
something with a lot of cream

I want to play on a fun team

I want to make Love and feel her as
she goes somewhere serene

Ever Dreamed

I speak and I dream and I Love as I do because I
feel within me the beating heart of those epic poems. No
matter how many thought me odd, or weak, or deluded
there is no chance in the recourse of my ways, of my
dreams. Who among us could ever, or would ever, shut
their eyes upon their bed and command that the things
within them that may spur amidst their slumber should
not be, though they were things that rendered what most
perceived to be the realities of waking life to dull dreams?
And how could one, even if they would, forget the power,
the awful beauty of dreaming when faced with a waking
that could not take a single breath were it not filled with
the air of dreams, of hopes, of desire for the quality of life,
in life; seen and felt and lived in dreaming, in speaking so
truly, in Loving and connecting so purely and profoundly?

And if not forgotten how could such dreams not burst
out into waking life in some form or another, at some time
and many after? But let us never forget, nor let those of
shallower experience render us disbelieving in the beauty
of life. Every tragedy may remain, and even therein may
be remembered; a thing that was before all else and lies

deeper than every tragedy and the deepest agony, a thing full of light. It is life that renders us to poetry, not poetry to simply dream away a dark life, but the beautiful miracles experienced in living; even betwixt the light and the dark, are in their clearer moments, things more wondrous to us than anything we have ever dreamed.

Forever Fall

Hearts burn

And lives learn

What it is to be truly happy

In each other's eyes we are madly

No longer do lonely hearts don faces so sadly

Because when I look at you

My heart does something new

And everything around me disappears

There is only our Love

And all that I thank above

There is only the most beautiful girl I have ever seen

There is no end to your sexy and serene

Hearts burn

And lips have no concern

For the saying of words at all

In Love with you I shall forever fall

Come Oh Love

Come oh Love and every beautiful emotion

Into this man's seeking motion

Moving fiercely towards that which is a man's honor

To seek with nature's devotion

Come oh girl of divine sexiness

Come with me to my bed

Whereupon I will place your elegant head

Let your fears be tranquil and few

Your curves and contours

Will never be dishonored by my eyes

But draped with passion and Loving wonder

By hands that eagerly wander

And eyes that ponder

How you could be so beautiful

Everything about you is a gift and a curse

For the gifts of your *assets* doom my days

The days you are not as close to me as possible

So look in my eyes withholding no sweetness

Nothing left guarded and nowhere left un-kissed

Receive my Loving lips upon your own

Into heaven I will make you sigh and moan

You will be my shore

And I your ocean

My passionate waves I will give to you

Until you are completely wet with pleasure

And upon the world we will lay

Breathless, serene, and joyous

Laughing into the sunlight

A Giant God

A giant god danced upon the primordial waters. With every step a thousand worlds were created in the ripples, and every time the god's eyes closed a thousand worlds were destroyed in the stillness. With every sacred movement the energies of creation were flung out and drawn back in. The giant god lived and died in every moment. Every moment contained the greatest passion and the most magnificent fulfillment. All was constantly pouring into and radiating out from the giant god. The dance was beautiful, the god felt pure joy, and the god saw only pure beauty in it all.

The giant god was of a pure mind, a mind disciplined by millions of years. In the beginning he was only a mind that became aware. There was nothing, and then he slowly emerged into a gradual awareness, until he became truly awake. And once awakened, you can imagine as if it were you; he was in awe of his own existence. His existence was solitary, but with his mind he could focus and produce anything he could imagine. Early on in his development things were more basic, but eventually he learned to focus only on positive thoughts and to then direct his will to the things he desired.

And after much time and desiring, as well as fearing, the giant god had created vast worlds full of life. But one day, as the giant god was playing upon the waters, the ripples and the beauty gave way to a light from out over their endless horizon. The light began to grow in power, beauty, and Lovingness. In a patient moment the light shown in full glory upon the giant god. Even amidst all that beauty and freedom the giant god was utterly baffled by the warm light, and the god knew that this Loving thing was worth giving up all things for. This all Loving energy, or consciousness was the source of all else, the source of his life, and he was a part of this light.

At War

I have been at war all of my life. Some others have viewed my life as being easy, as everything being handed to me. But I know the truth and as I sit here I shake my head. I just keep shaking my head and I smile and I feel the depths of my experience like a giant ocean moving within. I do not mean anyone any harm, but I am speaking to those who have harmed me with such views of myself, as well, to those who would harm any other being with their views; views that would rob them of depth, of pain, of immense suffering, of immense honor and beauty, of freedom, of respect and self-worth. I do apologize because I know there is more to you than the things you have shown me in your selves. However, your views are shallow and so shall your lives be, and every experience, and every relationship if you maintain such a shallow and disrespectful way of being. You are being shallow if you look at me and my life and think that it must be easy, that it must have been mostly easy, and full of mistakes. That perspective only shows how little you know of the depths of life.

I have been at war all of my life. I have fought. I have died…and died…and died. And my experience has shown me depths; depths that if you had seen you would not think and view as you do. You would not judge so harshly. And yet, you meander in front of me, you calmly sit in the luxurious filth you have surrounded yourself with. You smile, and you look at me, and you say words that do not understand a damn thing. And I am so thankful for that because you are wrong about me. And anyone like you will be wrong about many people.

Look…shallow people, or shallow views, would hurt you, but you don't need to listen to that crap. There are depths to life and even to those shallow people that none of us have any idea of, including myself. I am completely shallow before the infinite depths to life, to the idea and the beating heart of Love. But I will stand up for myself and for all those who do not believe that they have the strength to stand for their self. You all have that strength, you are all worthy of respect. No one needs me, or anyone else to stand up for them. So stand, and do not doubt the depths of your experience.

You Confuse

You confuse kindness in me for weakness,
and selfishness in yourself for strength

You think I am fraught with mistakes, but
you do not understand what it takes

To find the things in this life that you don't believe exist

You don't see all the harm you cause yourself and others

And you have no idea all that I have
accomplished and experienced

But that is okay

You can only take so much negativity from someone

Until

Their opinions of you cease to matter to you

And their approval becomes irrelevant

And then you free yourself to accept your own self

You confuse much about much

And yet you would say I'm out of touch

But I feel so much beauty

A great deal of what you see and feel is ugly

You would deny it

But you lie to others almost as much as to your self

And a puddle of mud may look great

Until

You see the ocean for the first time

And you realize

You never knew beauty

You only see what you are ready to see about me

You only see a muddied projection of yourself

And all the errors you think are in me are really in you

You confuse bad people for good ones

You confuse what is unpractical for practicality

You confuse emotional attachment and
some connection for truly deep Love

You confuse yourself most of all though
you consider yourself to be so clear

You confuse much about much

The Beers

The horror, the agony

The years, the fears

And the beers

The amazement, the laughter

The sunny days, the fun

And all the little happy moments

But let's still have a few beers

There are sober people in Tibet

I Pray

I pray to God, to all things…may I find happiness
within every day. I pray with all of my heart that this world
is given some real healing, that it is given some sort of gift
by God that will truly and deeply help it to revolutionize
itself. And I join with all those who ever have and ever
will pray the same sort of prayer. Let all our prayers for
ourselves, each other, and the whole world converge into

one stream of powerful light. And by the freedom of each individual will, let us send that light into the heart of heaven where it may ascend to and elicit the will of the Divine. Please God, give this world something so beautiful. You know what is in each of our hearts and souls; we ask to know what is in Yours. We ask to feel and experience such paradise in this life.

You Are

When you are one with God

When you experience that for whatever time is given to you

You are on that level

You are not below God reaching up

You are at your highest honor, and yet, you are dispersed

You are everywhere, in everything and
everyone, and you are nowhere

You are Loved

You Love

You are Love

You are perfect

All is light

Amaze You

I want to amaze you because I am amazed. I want to bring an energy through me that drops your jaws in awe. I want you to be awed by the power, the magic, the beauty, the profundity, and the purity of the energies we possess within our potential, even within our current kinetic. I do not want you to be awed by me really, but by what is in everything and everyone. But I must find it all in myself and balance my energy body in order to accomplish this. By energy body I mean the complete being that we all are. It may be expressed in different ways. In spiritual terms it refers to our chakras, our centers of energy and their corresponding energetic bodies. They include our physical body, our emotional body and our mental body, up to our divine body. In scientific terms it refers to our physical body composed of atomic energy fields, or particles, the electromagnetic radiation that we are as conscious organisms within a universe of light and matter. It is the full scope of our psychological relationship to every stimulus and experience in life; from our relationship to our bodies and emotions, to forgiveness and our understanding of ultimate reality, or self-realization.

All people possess the potential to experience levels of energy within their own minds and bodies that would utterly amaze them. Love is the feeling of infinity. The experience of Love is the experience of an endless emotion, it reveals to you rivers of pure emotion that run so deep within you that there is no end to them, and so you find that there is no end to you. You are not just this shallow physical being that is visible on the surface. And when Love is not felt it only lies asleep within the sanctuary of your heart. You will forever be safe within the sanctuary of God's heart. You will always be Loved, even when you don't feel it, even when you feel the opposite from everyone around you. And pure beauty will always be in your eyes, no matter how much ugliness you see with them. But seeing pain and ugliness has a beautiful purpose.

Your life and all of life is a miraculous gift. I have lost everything in myself and suffered beyond my limits, and I have also felt the suffering of years lift away. What a miraculous gift it all is! And what a horribly painful and confusing thing life can be! But the miracle is there. The beauty and the Love are there, one must seek them. One must want them. You will suffer and you will smile, but God willing your smiles will be sweeter because of the suffering; and your hearts and eyes will know the amazing gift life is, that Love is, that a girl is, or a boy is, and you are.

So much may fail, so much may hurt you, and make you feel so incomplete, but life will move on and I pray that such days and moments will come to you that sit you back and truly amaze you. Let them amaze you in such a way that you see the planning that went into your life, and all of what we think of as mistakes and tragedies may be seen for what they truly are; meaningful and powerful portions of a well lived life. Life, by its gift of a nature is impossible to live poorly; it may only be perceived in poor ways, or in richer ones. And most who would truly judge a life to be full of mistakes and poor choices focus their perception upon a very thin surface of life; and those sorts will remain judgmental, disrespectful, dishonest, unloving, and unamazed.

The Power

All leads back to the Source, to the alpha and the omega and so the journey in between is something very meaningful no matter what, and you might be surprised to realize the amazing journey certain choices of thought, of feeling, and of action can make for. There is power in this experience beyond knowing. The same power that has created this universe, and infinite more, flows through each and every being that will ever be upon any world or level of vibration.

Pain would not be if it were not for desire. The awesome power that is desire is what leads to all else for us; it leads to our growth, our joys, our fears, our failures, our successes, and to our beds for all else but sleep. Desire is what leads God to manifest consciousness into individualized portions autonomously desiring as their experiences co-create with them. Humans live! And they each are influenced by their environment and experiences toward their desires. The experiencing of all that is bad and undesired leads us further into the ever expanding frontier of desire. It is not necessary for us to experience the most horrible things in order to propel our development in some way, but there are so many more desires than you realize that you breathe out of you all the time. And the stronger and clearer your desire becomes the more painful your experience may be as well. A little desire may only lead to a little joy, or a little pain; the greater the desire the greater the potential for achieving great joy, and for achieving great sorrow. The level of pain and sorrow are a direct indication of the level of desire, and of the potential level of joy if you come to a more balanced place in yourself in order to more fully experience life as we are all capable of doing.

Through experiences that cause us any level of negative emotion we develop desires more powerfully, yes, but those more powerful negative experiences only exist because there was powerful desire preceding them. Without desire there is no pleasure or pain, there is no happiness or sadness because it would not matter to you. Pain and fear are but shadows of your desires, they are only capable of existing so long as the light of your desire shines within, and so long as you exist you will desire, but desires always lead to their fulfillment. It is inevitable, the power is too great, the potential for joy and fun and Love and sex is too important to us. And it should be, not because it has to be, but because we have felt the power, and we want more endlessly. What else could a heaven be if not at least unending powerful desire and unending pleasuring of every desire?

Rocky IV

This is my Rocky IV

I gotta hit the floor

And reach for the sky

There is not a thing I can afford to deny

Within me all will be accepted

In order to really get connected

To life

To my wife

Free from the past and its strife

It's for the strong of will

It takes heart to get up that hill

But we all need help up

And you have to ask to fill your cup

Ask for help from beyond physical

Who knows maybe there is something mystical?

In Times of Pain and Suffering

In times of pain and suffering I know there are no words that will take it all away. There is no understanding, no knowledge, or belief that will take away the pain.

When the heart breaks because someone Loved is lost to death or the end of a relationship we feel that pain run deep within. When great tragedy and difficulty comes for whatever reason we are bound to suffer. The point is not to simply remove pain and suffering; that is not all that healing is about. Healing will come in time. It is as inevitable as the withering cold of winter will in time hail the sun's rise from that wintery death, and through the natural course of time, return to your hemisphere bringing the resurrection of warmth and life. Just as the seasons pass over this world, so too may your light fade from you in winter, but there is a rhythm to life worth believing in, and you may behold the return of your light as a new season comes.

The pain is powerful, but that power can only last so long in clear form. It may linger for years, but it will change, and fade, and so long as you find some peace with what has been, in time it will heal. It is an amazing and deep experience. It is worthy of your honor and amazement that you are capable of such pain. Believing that there is reason and purpose may not take it away, but it can bring you peace amidst suffering; it may be a guide to you when you are so lost. And when the heart breaks it is of great value for you to believe that nothing needs to stop you from Loving, or from believing that this life may be able to show you reasons to Love your life again, or even for the first time. The heart is the center of our being, and when it is in harmony you are capable of feeling like this life is paradise. I have felt that amidst deep suffering. I know that we can feel both. We can suffer to the ends of us, and we can believe in it, and we can feel great reverence, peace, and Love amidst our tragedies. Of course, when the deeper parts of your trauma are fresh you will not feel paradise within, but after some time, while the suffering is still strong enough, you may know horrible pain and deep peace in the same moment.

To those who pass over into life beyond we may focus great Love. We may let them be free to move onward, not that they are gone forever, but we may honor and respect their freedom from this flesh, from being here in physical form with us. They are always with us, and we with them, and we will one day be with them again to experience more things than the minds of men believe. Talk to them in your mind, and know that anything you think may be sent to them and they will receive it, they are aware of your energy, especially of the energy you send to them, that you think about them. You may aid them by letting them be free, by respecting the free will of their soul to be in life, or to be in life beyond. And it is a great service that you may give to them to allow them their freedom, to continue to give them your Love and forgiveness.

In times of truly deep pain and suffering you will have ups and downs. Things will get better in time, and my heart goes out to you, but it will of course take more time than you would like. You would like there to be no pain, and no event or reality that caused you to suffer, you would deeply desire for whatever occurred to be reversed. But it will be important in time for you to realize that you may find great happiness, peace, and forgiveness for all without it being reversed, no matter what it is. The deepest pains will break your heart; they will break your belief that there could be any good for you while such a thing has happened. It is this belief that you must break in time; because no matter what happens you can find happiness again. No matter who or what you have lost you are capable of finding great Love and happiness again. And it is the nature of suffering that, if given enough time, your being is affected in ways that produce the potential within you to be happier than ever before. It is the nature of suffering to lead you into deep and remarkable change, growth, and power within yourself. As weak as you may feel, the experience is a truly powerful one, and that experience is a part of you, it may only exist to the extent of your depths. Without you it is gone. But within you worlds may shatter, hells may be endured, and heavens may be formed from the destruction.

That may sound ridiculous, but I stand by it. And of course I am speaking of potentialities. Individuals may believe many different things, some may take things more positively and others more negatively. You may seek healing, or you may seek self-destruction. You may believe it is meaningful, or that it is meaningless. If it is meaningful there is healing in that alone, as well as incentive to seek further healing, and further meaning. If it is meaningless then all the more reason to strive for healing, to rid yourself of what is unnecessary and move on. Love is the key. Love is at the heart of it all, at the source of heartbreak, and at the center of what it is to be healed, and to be a healer.

You may wander about as if in a desert for years, seeking this and that, whatever you think may bring you happiness, whatever you feel you must, or that you need and want, but until you seek and find Love in your heart for...for all that you can, and for yourself, true and deep healing will evade you. All that your life can be will lie within, untapped, unknown, and unimagined until you open up your heart and really start believing in so much more beauty to this powerful and perfect existence we share with one another; this existence that may send your mind unto the depths of infinity, to an awareness of the fact that you are not just this body, this personality, that there is a deep ocean of calm, peaceful, powerful, joyous, and Loving beingness beneath all that surface life; there is infinite life living within and you may dive down to know what it is to be complete, to be whole, perfect, and free from all pain and fear. In times of pain and suffering there are no limits to the good that may come from your experience.

The Heart

God created all that there is from Her own divine light, with the Love and care of His own immaculate heart. Though there are so many other forms of life, humanity is a great feat for creation; created as such for a purpose, with meaning, and artistic genius. And yet, humanity possesses a judgmental nature, which deems so much of its own nature to be unacceptable, undesirable, and unwise. But we are as we are as a result of the evolution of a universe that has taken about 14 billion years to this point in time. As humans we cannot see the half of it; the consciousness of infinite wisdom has mentally produced a universe full of complex systems of energy and life on such an extraordinary scale. It is absolutely unintelligible to the human mind. It is only through the human heart that the Truth may become clear. The heart reveals the sanctity of all human experience. In the heart one may join the flow of all creation and realize that all is occurring perfectly. All pains will be healed, and every injustice will be set right, is right now.

His Answering

I lie down on my floor

Like I used to when I was hurting so deep

I would go outside and lie on the concrete

Just looking up at the sky and those stars

Pouring everything out to everything there is

But now there is a new resolve

There is me and the evening light

Me and the trees and the calm breeze

Birds and flourishing life everywhere

We are so alive and we seek the light

Together we join and soar with joy

Screaming, singing, laughing, and looking

THE FATES, THE POWER, AND THE GREAT JOY

Looking to the Creative Principle

To the depths of our selves where we are whole

And bursting with Love, power, and peace

The Power

The Life within

The Desire

And the passion for more

The rest of the world sees itself more a dying thing

A weak, wrong, tragic thing that is so dirty

So undeserving of Love and great power

And of the great gift of sexuality

They make avenues for an often cheap and debasing act

There is so much more to life and fucking

Every tragedy and every sexual act

Are a sharing and combining of powerful energies

A sharing of our entire being

There is so much more to absolutely everything

That if all was known

That is, if you experienced your energy in full

There would be no fear, no incompletion anywhere

And an overwhelming experience of self-
respect, Love, Peace, and Understanding

I understand there is great suffering

So much of the world calls out for help

There are countless prayers rising
from all those who suffer

And each call rises up to our Totality

The Creator has heard everyone

It feels the will of every single soul

And in your deepest pleas for God's help

Such beauty is seen to rise and to fall

Rising from the call for hope back down to despair

But the Creator has hands of air

Gentle hands that would have you know their intimate care

Oh how they care for you

For each and every one of you

The Creator has long answered these calls

The wills of great masses effects the will of the One

And His response reverberates back to this hurting world

The manners in which He has done so are not apparent

But He has not concluded His answering

Space/Time and Time/Space

Throughout history there is a common theme: there
exists a consensus understanding of reality that is

wrong, at least in some fundamental or poignant way. Then improvements come about, or more accurate developments in our understanding of existence in any regard. But the mainstream, or consensus, rebukes such movements and their understandings until the proper time in which the old ways of understanding fall away and new understandings are accepted as true laws, or descriptions of reality. I accept the fact that all of my views may be completely wrong, but I also enjoy the fact that they may constitute any degree of accuracy no matter how many so called experts would disagree. Our experts have always been wrong about much, and our consensus fights and frowns against almost every development in our understanding of reality.

That said, the following is somewhat of an initial response, or reaction within myself, to the reciprocal system theory posited by Dewey B. Larson. My mind does not perceive any true division between science and spirituality, so my thoughts always seek to understand the two together, or at least parallel to one another. In my opinion, Larson provides a concise scientific understanding of our physical universe and should be given any good credit, if any were to be given, for what I attempt to express herein. However, I do not claim to fully understand his theories, thus my apologies to the reader and to Dewey. And also, please forgive me for being repetitious but it is like playing a song, you need a chorus to really express it within yourself and create connections of thought, and in this case I wanted to be able to hit things at different angles, different ways of wording things. Forgive me as well for the abrupt correlation that I make between physical scientific realities and spiritual ones, but they are one in the same, in my opinion. Of course, there is a great deal I do not understand well enough to put more simply, clearly, and eloquently, but I offer what I may.

Atoms and photons are essentially equivalent in that they are each discrete units of space/time which are displaced from the regular motion of space and time. Allow me to try to elaborate. Space/time is one thing, and it is the unity of all energy. Space and time are reciprocal in nature, otherwise stated that they are expressions of one another that exist in tandem and combine to express a single whole. They are mirror images of one another and the two images are both mere reflections of something else. They are refractions of a single source of light. You might say that space is the physical manifestation of time. And time is essentially just the manner in which the universe expresses an analog for infinity itself.

As such, space and time are infinite because they are expressions of infinity. Imagine time as a thing that is in motion. This is not too difficult because it is easily accessible in our everyday experience; you are breathing right now in this moment, and then the next, and then the next, and so on and so forth. It is always moving at the same rate of speed, it is regularized, not your breathing, but the movement of time. Now, space itself is always moving as well. The universe is seen to be expanding due to this phenomenon. The space in between everything is constantly expanding, just as time is constantly expanding, or moving at a certain rate of speed. Electromagnetic energy fields of coalescence (matter) formed within the expansion of space/time introduces alterations within the physics of their local environment. Outwardly the expansion seeks and expresses infinity even in increasing momentum from the speed of light to supra-luminal and approaching the paradox of infinite velocity of a single particle moving so fast through space and time that it is every particle that has ever been beyond speed and time...it is now all that is and ever was, one particle, one moment, infinite and forever. Inwardly the gravitation of mass seeks and expresses infinity in equal and opposite velocity and gaining of momentum unto infinity within a singularity; infinite mass, infinite density, infinite time.

Amidst this infinite space/time the universe manifests a certain amount of matter, or energy, occurring in various processes and manifestations in certain amounts of time. That is, there exists all the different particles and elements that coalesce into stars and planets and these manifestations occur, or evolve throughout periods of time. So, throughout infinite space/time particles exist because their motion somehow becomes de-regularized from the regularized motion of space/time itself. What we have then is a universe that is constituted by the various harmonies of motion between space and time. Balance between these motions would describe what we would see as empty space. It is basically the same concept as two objects moving in the same direction, parallel to one another, and at the same rate of speed. If you were on one of the objects the other object would appear to stand still. Yet another helpful analogy is the T-Rex in "Jurassic Park." In the movie, the dinosaur could only perceive motion. When the people stood still it could not perceive them. Our perception of the universe is basically a combination of these two analogies.

What I mean is that we only perceive motion just like the T-Rex, but space/time itself is in constant motion. We do not perceive it in the same way as we do visible physical phenomena in the universe because of its regularized rate of motion. This employs the first analogy of the two objects moving parallel at the same rate. I understand this analogy is not entirely accurate since the reality is more nuanced, but it is difficult to describe these things. Nonetheless, I imagine the clearest possible communication of our cosmology is simple.

Empty space is analogous to our perception of objects moving at the same rate, thus we perceive there to be no motion, and without motion there is no light or visible energy because space and time are existing in perfect unity, in perfect reciprocity. Like the T-Rex, we only perceive the motion of portions of space/time that are moving, and moving in a different way than the regularized motion of space/time. This de-regularized motion we perceive as light and matter, as the photon and the atom. Therefore, we have come full circle in expressing what should be very simple, and yet, may seem to be so complex because I fail to both communicate and understand these things more clearly.

In order to recapitulate and expand these understandings...there is harmony. Space/time is in motion. It is motion; it only perceivably exists because it is in motion. There is the infinite progression, or expansion, of space and time and there is the inward movement of gravitation, which is simply an inversion of the expanding motion. But what we normally perceive in the universe is motion that is de-regularized. What we perceive is space/time moving against the current, or at a different velocity as the rest of space/time. We understand these perceptions of the dis-unity of space/time as the photon and the atom, and thus as motion. This motion, angular velocity, or vibration creates light, and light produces further compound movements upon its initial vibration and coalesces to create everything in the physical universe.

The outward expanding movement is like a forever moving straight line occurring in a single dimension of motion. The photon takes this foundational motion and adds another dimension of movement, an oscillation, or vibration, thus manifesting two dimensions of motion, and these particles are carried by the expansion of space, thus the speed of light is simply the rate of expansion of space/time itself. The atom is a unit of space/time manifesting three dimensions of motion, and instead of being carried by that outward movement, it "gravitates" inward and moves backwards along the progression of space/time. Atoms and matter are not attracted to each other by the force of gravity; instead, gravity is simply their individual movements opposite the space/time progression; it is movement inward like a reverse explosion. In a spiritual sense, gravity is the will to seek the inward spiraling line of light to the source. There are also four, five, six, seven, and eight dimensional units of space/time, which manifest their respective dimensions of motion and correspond to levels of total mass and thus gravity.

Moving onward, matter in the universe is the result of our perception of fields of energy forming foci, luminal aggregates, or groupings of elements due to gravity, and gravity is the relationship between the motion of atoms and the motion of space/time. Gravity is like water moving up the windshield of a car while it is going very fast. A single drop of water will flow up the windshield, and we could say that there is a force that causes water to flow up, or backwards across the windshield. But the true force at work is the movement of the car in the opposite direction as it causes the water to flow. The force with which the water flows up is a result of the movement in the other direction, and of course the amount of water. Gravity is the inversion of expansion moving matter inward toward the nucleus, and toward every other nucleus because space/time is constantly expanding outward in every direction. The inward regression of gravity and the outward moving progression of space/time are really the same energy, or motion, manifesting a reciprocal relationship, or at least an apparently opposite one. They are inverse expressions of one whole. They are the fundamental movements of space and time; the outward movement toward expansion and the inward movement back toward the source.

There is only the motion of space/time. The photon and the atom are discrete units of space/time that move in such a way that, when they are combined with many more units of displaced space/time, they create the illusion of matter and light. They create the illusion of constancy and lack of motion when the reality is anything but. Our scientists have examined photons and atoms and found that they are primarily empty. What they find are the effects of motion. They find a series of electromagnetic disturbances that exist as a result of the displacement of space/time from moving in perfect unison. It is de-regularized from the regular movement. This possesses exciting consequences, or realities.

All that exists in the physical universe comes from, and forms itself out of, a nebulous reality of pure energy, or motion within numerous dimensions. There are only disturbances and manifestations of a unified energy that are perceivable. Imagine that there is nothing in existence; go back to the beginning and try to imagine it. Back before stars, planets, galaxies, the photon, and the atom. There is only the emptiness of infinite space and time. But what are space and time at this point? They mean nothing. There is only a nebulous infinity. There is nothing to exist and move in whatever space is. There are no people to go to work for eight hours each day and to live throughout the years. What is space? What is time? In and of themselves they are empty and infinite. There is just an endlessness. Out of that infinite emptiness, and/or that plenum...there is mystery...there is a miracle because something exists.

All that exists in the universe known to man are distortions in the unity of space/time. These disturbances, distortions, displacements, and/or de-regularizations are essentially perceivable to us as the atom and the photon, which are really the same thing with different amounts of movement, vibratory and rotational velocity, and thus, different electromagnetic properties. Space/time is displaced from perfect reciprocity, from unity, and flung out into existence. It basically attempts to rejoin, or is drawn back toward that state of unity. Therefore, all things come out of infinite unity and evolve, or revolve, back to unity once more. However, the displacements are so small they must coalesce. They must group together in order to gain enough energy, mass, and/or gravity to re-enter unity. Photons and atoms are too small to collapse under their own gravity, thus balancing the ratio of space/time and forming a black hole, or singularity. It is the trip from space/time to time/space, from physical to metaphysical, and physics all its own.

Gravity is the measurement of space/time ratios (ratios that have more space or more time). It is a measurement of their attraction toward that state of unity. And that state of unity is the Divine. It is the One Infinite Creator of Love and Light. We all feel that attraction; that pull, that ancient calling back toward unity. But we are mere individual souls; we are so small upon the wayside of infinite unity. And so we amass experience, we develop our energy, we seek a higher and higher rotational velocity. Our gravity grows while we coalesce, and every life within the evolution of energy that is a soul combines to create a euphonious song.

Our souls group together to form metaphysical aggregates of energy: just as stars group within galaxies, and the galaxies themselves start spinning into spirals of stellar beauty; higher and higher the galaxies ascend the path of light back to the unity of all energy; souls develop their energies in the same way, group together, and ascend the evolutionary path toward their own completion. So, whether it is a galaxy of stars, or of souls, the spiral arms wrap around tighter and tighter as we move faster and faster. And then, it is accomplished. All is released into God's sacred beingness in a flash of all consuming light. It is unified. It is infinite. No space. No time. No you or me...Only perfect harmony, power, Love, wisdom, and yet, an abiding aura of mystery, the unknown and unknowable depths to our infinite unified Self.

Therefore, I see no true divide between science and spirituality. They are each describing the same things with a different vocabulary. They each seek to understand the great evolution of energy that has taken place in our existence. There are simply many things that we have yet to clearly understand, and when we do the pieces will fall together and form a single beautiful picture of life. But I could be wrong about everything, I don't think I am, but I could be, and most likely am to some degree about some things herein.

So what all this means for us on earth is that we are part of a vast evolution, and in my opinion, that evolution not only occurs in terms that science has thus far been prepared to face, but in what we call spiritual terms as well. I think that the physical manifestations of evolution within existence, such as space/time, particles, molecules, cells, organisms, species, civilizations, planets, stars, galaxies, and universes are a part of this spiritual evolution. They are each a part of one another. It is just that right now none of us see what happens after we die, or higher frequencies of light, of thought, and emotional states. Higher stages of evolution are cut off from our conscious perception and so it is natural for us to think that there is nothing more than human life for us. Our human eyes only perceive the tiny sliver that is the visible spectrum of light. Look at all that this universe has manifest in just a physical form. My God it is enormous! It contains such order, harmony, beauty, and mystery. And I desire for you all to have a better understanding of your place in that wonderful existence; in this evolution that your soul is embarked upon. I desire for you to be highly skeptical of limits to understanding, of limits to perception of reality, of limits to the worth of your fellow man, and of limits to your potential, even your destiny beyond a single human life, beyond space and time.

I Remember

I remember the day that wind touched my face

And I stopped right in my place

It changed my life

It was a truly rare moment

When God speaks and you understand

When some sort of grace takes your hand

And you know that there is more than what we see

And you know there is more than pain to life

It's been almost ten years since that day

And I sit where I sat before

THE FATES, THE POWER, AND THE GREAT JOY

And there is a gentle breeze

My oh my it fills me with such ease

My oh my how completely I desire Love

It has been years since I had that dream

The one that showed me into the future

The one in which we meet

I pray so deeply for that day to finally come

And today the wind touches my face

And I stop in my place

There is a beautiful calm all around me

And I dream of she

My oh my I could never say how much it will mean to me

To see her face

To look into her eyes

And to kiss her lips

To feel her in my heart from the very start

It has been years since that day

One I will never forget

When all of my sight was filled with light

And my heart felt full of Love

And there was no fear

Only God

My oh my how deeply I desire to understand

The Creator, this creation, and myself

I desire and I seek with everything in me

Love

Without Love

I am constantly down low praying to above

It is Love

It is in my heart

It is in her eyes

She is in my dreams

She is in my wake

There is so much Love to her I want to make

The Dancing Devil

A devil danced before the Divine One and spoke
unto Her and said, "Your virginal stupidity knows not of
the truth, you are a weak, unworthy fool, and I will make
you shake and cower when I show you my world." And
the devil said every horrible thing to Her; he told Her of
every perversion, every crime against another, and of
all that was stupid and wrong about all she knew, all that
She believed. And when the devil had exhausted every
frightening thing and every argument he stepped back and
smiled in his victory. But then, the devil sought to access

the true state of his adversary. He looked into Her eyes and realized they blinked not once during his whole attack.

He felt Her energy feel all that he had expressed, and She, you could say accepted it all, but it's far more than that. She found Love for everything, for him, and for every wrong that could ever be in anything and anyone, even Herself. She had peace in light of every disharmony. And then, as the devil continued to gaze into Her eyes, She showed him the feeling of true peace with infinite power. And then she showed him true disharmony with infinite power, and wisdom, and unity, and faith, and joy, and sadness, and fear all with that power, and then a bigger picture that included all those things. And the devil fell to his knees and wept. Everything in him flooded out to all things, and all things returned to him an enlightenment; a purified mental/emotional state of being that made the heavy physical body a light thing. And the deeper heaviness at the heart of one who felt himself a devil became a shining light of angelic beauty.

Nothing But Bless

Relax

Go slow and enjoy the show

Let every single thing go

I do not know

But I don't want to feel low

And I don't want to always hear the word no

Yes

I don't want to always feel like less

I must confess

Amidst all this perceived mess

There is a reality that does nothing but bless

The hearts and minds of those who guess

There is way more within human eyes than we profess

At the center of every galaxy

Black holes absorb all the light

At the center of every eye is a black hole

Letting in all the light

Chakras

Chakras are essentially your soul as it exists at a certain point in space/time, or in your evolution as a soul. And your soul is a manifestation of a single spark of the Creator. Your soul is a manifestation and a vessel for God. And your body is a manifestation and a vessel for your soul, your energy body, or your chakral system.

You may not believe that the body possesses these energy centers, but even if this is the case the principles to do with the chakras provide a clear and workable model for finding psychological well-being. Beginning with the root chakra we are faced with establishing a feeling of safety and a healthy relationship with our physical bodies. We are thus faced with the needs and desires of our bodies, which must be given equal respect as the highest of energies, desires, or needs. It is about finding a healthy way to treat ourselves in every aspect that we are.

The Buddha

The Buddha had been sitting in meditation for hours. He felt a great calm, a slowness, and that sweet feeling that arises from elevated and purified emotions. And as he opened his eyes a smile stretched across his lips. Nature was all around him and the sounds of it were like musical notes touching deep in his heart with every vibration upon the air. He had experienced the pleasures of earthly life in abundance, and for some time he had renounced that life to seek the truth; he sought the resolution to all suffering and his focus was fierce.

One Universe

There is one universe, but it exists at potentially infinite other portions of time/space. Within our current orientation of space/time we would consider there to be many universes existing within the same basic space, but occurring in our past and future. All the stars and galaxies are like the chakras of the Infinite Self, and the universe in totality is essentially the 8th chakra freely flashing its pure white light and resting within its energy in harmonic intervals. It is music, it is beautiful in the eyes of God, and it is paradise in our unified heart. Every level of vibration of light, every dimension, even infinite energy exists in a single space, in a single moment.

We exist in a continuum that goes from space/time to time/space, then to space/time in the next creation, octave of experience, or universe. The motion of all things is that of an upward rising spiral; it is in our DNA, it is in the photons, it is in the atoms, it is in the planets, and stars, and galaxies, and universes. Our space/time is constantly being supplied the completion of the aggregations in the previous creation from its time/space portion. These particles are dispersed throughout space and they evolve into denser and denser aggregates, such as atoms, stars, and galaxies. Then that evolution comes to the completion of aggregation in space/time and is transferred into time/space, where the particles are dispersed throughout time as opposed to space. Then those particles coalesce and form denser and denser aggregates in time/space; until they reach the completion of aggregation in time and spiral upward to be transferred to the space/time of an higher octave of experience, creation, or universe. This describes the basic evolution of matter in space and time, as well as of souls.

Souls of energy evolve through three dimensions of space, or physical manifestations of being, and three dimensions of time, or spiritual manifestations of being. Our energy begins its evolution as the elemental material of physical manifestation in the first dimension; this includes the beingness of space/time itself, then particles you could say, of increasing complexity and energy, and in time elements complete this foundational cycle by achieving awareness after experiencing the catalyst of chaos, or random action upon dormant conscious beingness. The second dimension of manifestation is what we consider plant and animal life; the nature of nature being to seek growth, to seek the light unto further awareness. The first dimension of the evolution of consciousness sees it go from unconscious being to achieving consciousness on a fundamental level. The second dimension is a higher level of conscious awareness beginning more generally then increasing and culminating in complex mind and body relationships of animals, such that, self-awareness is achieved with consistency, no longer so instinctual through the awareness of its group mind.

The third is as we experience now, consciousness at the level of humanity, in which what we would consider an individual soul is achieved and able to begin its free evolution. Upon reaching a certain level within its evolution a soul is prepared to enter the fourth dimension, which is the first of the spiritual dimensions of time/space. At a further point the second spiritual dimension is entered, and then the third; these levels of being may also be understood as the fifth and sixth dimensions of our evolution. There is also a seventh dimension wherein the totality of being is experienced. And finally, every soul enters the eighth dimension which also serves as the first dimension in its latter portion for the next octave of evolution, or the next universe of creation. Grain of salt anyone?

The Meaning

What is the meaning of life? My mind pauses and then, I think to God; what does it mean to Him? But the way I see it, God is all that there is for God; the infinite dimensions of light and life fall into that heart and all that is left is the One. The Creator must answer for Himself. What life means becomes what does God mean to God? If you were the only thing in existence, then what you determined to be your meaning would be essential. But no matter what you determined to be so, there is every meaning and no meaning; we are beyond meaning in such a way that leaves us completely releasing ourselves into the mystery of it all. But why exactly? Is that what a girl asks herself during a great orgasm? Why may be intriguing, but when it is experienced the why and the meaning are inseparable from the experience itself. It is an orgasm.

Just the same you can ask what the meaning of life is, but the total experience of it, which includes many, many lives, is an experience which cannot be separated from and defined against a meaning. You can give a biological and spiritual meaning to the experience itself, but that is more a description of how and not a true understanding of why. The meaning to life is so intimately intertwined with the experience; however, this understanding is not as readily accessible as the analogy of an orgasm because we only see a single life. We do not have available to us the totality of our experience. When that totality is seen and felt I promise you that it is an orgasmic experience that leaves no lack of meaning, nothing unfulfilled, and only pure joy.

Art

If you become good enough at something, or if there is true appreciation for something then it becomes art. Sex can be an art, and you can be an artist in bed, or wherever the passion takes you. I seek to create beautiful art that communicates what it is to be alive, at least for myself. Any art only comes as a reflection and expression of the experience of living. It is art because life is art; it is artistic, and moving, and full of energies to be released from within that are beautiful.

Spirit of Humanity

I am a spirit, a soul, inhabiting this sphere across its brief billions of years of time. I have seen many things, many that you have forgotten. I know many things, many that you have known merely as a soft breeze upon your faces, and then its knowledge has vanished in the stillness of time. I have walked with your masters, many men and women once Loved, then made into gods and many forgotten still of those divine souls. I have looked into Jesus' eyes during his most happy moments, and I looked through them during their most painful hour. I have welcomed our friends from other planets and stars, and I have felt their Love and beauty. I have fought in every human war upon earth and I have known pain and fear beyond my measure. I have travelled to every mountain top to stand and see what it could give to me, and I have felt the energy of God flow through me to give to all things. I have sat in the shadows of light during the most secret meetings of men, and I have been honored to hear the angels sing of all that this earth is destined for. I have stood before the council of nine and reveled in their vibrations. I have released all of me to realize all that is; the self, poured out into Infinity and sent back...to be, to be free, to be happy, to breathe air and look through eyes, to stare in adoring wonder at all that I have seen and remember; to stand upon memories secure and strong, and to call forth desires for endless more.

Empires

Empires rise and empires fall

The chorus is sung and we can hear the call

Let the truth rise from within the mind

True history of this world is tough to find

THE FATES, THE POWER, AND THE GREAT JOY

It is kept from us and so the blind lead the blind

And we say we see

The chorus is sung and we sing "My country tis of thee"

Our truest patriots were free and righteous dissenters

But now they are obedient and violent defenders

The drama builds, the subtext goes by unread

The truth is tough to find when you
can't afford your daily bread

All the while an enormous story goes by unseen by most

And the earthly powers that be make a toast

To all their money and power

They see themselves as wise kings and
you all but stupid ants to tower

Over and over until you cower

In so much fear, self-doubt, and lowly
hopes that you would enslave

Your selves to these masters instead of being brave

But brave can be many things

It may be resigned to expanding your understandings

Revolutions are not all won with guns
and declarations to the tyrannical

They may be individual and internal

A place no one can ever truly control

A truth no lie can distort because it's in your heart and soul

And until you more truly dissent from
your fears and negativity

You shall be slaves to your own inner tyranny

All the while the powers that be do not see

The things that are beyond their fear based plans

The plans of much greater powers than mans'

Empires rise and empires fall

The chorus is sung and we can hear the call

The plans of nature are not easily lied to

Nor do they fear what any level of beings may do

There is nothing to fear

We are all here

With great plans of our own

We are creators not just made of blood and bone

Living lights of the creative force

That force, that thought, that idea, that belief, that

Conscious and all powerful meditative
enlightenment that came as a miracle

Love

Love is the creative force

The principle upon and through which all radiates

All of creation is riding that wave

And no matter how this world will behave

THE FATES, THE POWER, AND THE GREAT JOY

No plan of man can compete with the creative force

The infinite waters will follow their own course

Nature knows of power and secrets as old as time

The current empire must have forgotten the rhyme

The rhythm and the dance of our natural creation

Will lead all things unto complete liberation

And the history of humanity will finally be free

From war, injustice, and tyranny

So sound the call

Empires are destined to fall

And we need not any action at all

Save the search within to break down every wall

Separating each of us from our own right to be happy

It may be a little sappy

But Love and joy are inside of you to find

And when more of us do

Then our social structures will begin
to reflect it back to you

Just look within to find your own peace

We can see a day when fear and hate will cease

The chorus is sung and we can hear the call

Empires rise and empires fall

As Humans

As humans we can only see the visible spectrum of light with our eyes. And yet, we think that we see so much nowadays. We think we understand our world so well. We use such a small percentage of our brains, but our scientists know everything, or at least most of it now... civilization is quite advanced right?

I don't think so. We have come very far, but there is so much more in us, around us, and up there. I do believe in an energy; the source of all life that exists everywhere at all times. I believe in the infinite beauty of an emotion, a living state of being that is completely aware on levels that are hardly comprehensible to one in a human state of being. I believe in the existence of Love, which is a description of the ultimate reality and origin of all things; the origin to everything in the physical universe is a state of being, an essence, a non-physical scientifically understandable reality, an intelligent emotional power of a joyous and benevolent nature. It is the Truth because It is the source, the ultimate, the conscious creator, facilitator, and harvester of all existence. It is deeply kind, warm, beautiful, hopeful, and fearless. It is complete. It has will. It manifests infinite processes and individualized intelligences that may generally be understood as an all-encompassing evolution intended to give self-knowledge to the Creator. An evolution of: electromagnetic energies, particles, elements, species, planets, stars, souls, civilizations, galaxies, and universes. And the tiniest microcosm is completely connected to the largest macrocosm; every microcosm extends from the whole and manifests frequencies that may harmonize with the source vibration. As humans I dare say that we do not understand much of what is going on in this evolution, let alone within ourselves.

We Were Young

We were young when we met

And she began breaking my heart at the onset

I can't really blame her though

How could either of us know

Our young lives had too much pain

To fall in Love and not go insane

Innocent babes born unto a harsh world

And parents whose troubles unfurled

Upon our more sensitive constitutions

They couldn't give us what they didn't
have in themselves, restitutions

So much that no one could see

Girl of my past we

Were meant to be what we were

Others have hurt you deeply but I confer

We were never victims

But our healing will require more than singing hymns

Think I'm stupid, think I'm crazy for all I say

But there may come a day

When you will want to be truly healed

That is the very purpose our lives concealed

Why do you think we suffered so?

Just so hell could open and heaven could say no?

Just so young hearts could want to be happy

Only to always watch everything go crappy?

Nothing special about this life is there?

Mostly pain and fear and beer and bills and debt

And where the hell did anything good and right go?

Until you die

And all you can do is try

And fail to fly

And scream why

No

All can be healed in everyone

And even the most cold and serious can have some fun

Have a little hope

There is a great deal of spirituality way beyond the pope

All that unsexy attire needs must retire

THE FATES, THE POWER, AND THE GREAT JOY

And melt in Love's freeing fire

There is a way

No matter what they say

To heal all things

To awaken to what your life constantly sings

And all the angelic beings

It can happen for you

The greatest things can happen

If any but would be more and more open

Open in mind as well as in heart

If you could just be understanding

There are infinite possibilities

But let me be clear girly

Even though I have moved on surely

I will always Love you

I deeply desire for you to be happy

Truly Loved and fulfilled by your own self and by your life

And even though you were always good

At blocking me from your heart and mind

I believe that you will always have Love
inside yourself for me as well

Freedom

Freedom...Freedom of thought, of opinion, of perception; what other principle so openly demonstrates the capacity of Love? To really allow people to be free, and see a deeper worth in them for all that they are no matter what, that is to honor freedom. If you go at a situation already thinking you need to change someone in some way then there is not full honoring of freedom.

Freedom is wise. It may seem a chaotic theory, but it finds an order that is pure and directly in its own direction toward what we all seek. Of course, we will disagree with one another, with many others, and agree with enough as well, but no matter because we are free. We may have disagreements and emotional reactions because it means something to us, but no matter. Let it matter, and let it fall away. Let hate, and anger, and fear, and let understanding for the self and the other be seen. And then you can let Love for what is, and peace within, and positive desires flood over you. Let it all happen. Let all things naturally be thought, felt, desired, undesired, agreed with, and disagreed with; let it all be and accept, forgive, and Love it all in you. You are a natural and pure being just as you are. You are not defined by sin, not in my opinion; even there are no mistakes. All is given to the Creator, to the harvest of existence.

Anyway

You can see things anyway you want. Some people have thought that I am stupid, and others that I am smart. Some have thought of me extremely negatively, and others extremely positively. To some the things I think, say, and feel seem pretty gay, to others they only seem a little gay. Some would call me evil, and others would call me angel. To some I am ugly, and to others I am very attractive. So what am I? Well, I obviously can't simply listen to the many fickle voices of others concerning me or else I would be constantly torn back and forth from one end of the spectrum to the other. I can understand any opinion and perception, but no one knows me and no one knows you unless they Love you as a perfect being just the way you are. I think of myself as a living extension of the one consciousness that is all that is and that we are all a part of. Anything else is merely what I would think of this individual being among an infinite sea of perfect beings recapitulating the evolution of God's expanding consciousness through the evolution of their expanding souls.

Ima Tell You

Ima tell you how It's been

Your sweet earth has seen so much

Pain, violence, and darkness

And for all this there has been great power amassed

Awaiting the will of man to unite

Ima tell you how it's gonna be

You're gonna give your Love for free

Unconditionally

Honor and respect to all

And when you do

Your lives and your planet

Will come to life

Like a dull dream has been your sleep

And now

You will awaken

If you really want to

It 's only kinda crazy

It is not a lie

No one will ever die

I Have a Dream

I have a dream that one day this world will be truly happy. I dream of a time when no one has to work, when there is no rent, or utilities, or taxes. I dream of free clean renewable energy; a healthier planet and healthier people. I dream of a day when all the governments, and religions, and races drop all the old definitions that would separate us and our perceptions of the Source of all there is, within all there is. I dream of a day when all beings are seen as worthy, amazing, and free. I have a dream of a spiritual revolution that wakes up the world to unconditional respect to all beings, all times, all emotions, and all experiences. I have a dream that more and more see that we are creators, that we are energy and vibration, and that our will, thoughts, and emotions are responsible for what comes to us. I dream of the day when truly Loving aliens mass land and walk with us hand in hand. I dream of a world free from its fears. It is a world without: wars, weapons, money, pollution, crime, prisons, disease, and the religions of old. It is a world where everyone is happy, where everyone knows that all deserve the respect of a fellow creator. I dream of a world where people are much more focused on feeling Love, having fun, and truly understanding our infinite creation. I dream this dream and I know it is inevitable.

In Life

In life, in existence, we may feel so alone, so separated from all else, but the truth is absolutely contrary. We are, and all is, one organism if you will. We are all like sprouts of life above ground, each free to dance with the wind in our own free space, but if you go down below the surface, you will find that we all share a common root structure. We are all the same living thing. And our life is held up by a single thought, by a single truth that may be summed up in two words: I Love. There is a deep running bond between all things that possesses such a pure and beautiful mental/emotional nature. It is the emotional bond we share with one another, and with ourselves, that truly connects us to life, breathes life into us, and makes our free space feel like a beautiful dance instead of a lonely prison.

Countless Angels

I do not regret the things that have caused me to suffer. They were not mistakes, they absolutely were not. There is a lot of cool shit going on in creation. It does not have to matter what others think of you, or believe about you. And all others may Love you, but if you don't Love you then what is it worth to you? You don't know a thing about you if you don't Love you. You are more than your actions in one life, or your possessions, or your dirtiest confessions. There are countless angels looking at you, and smiling at you in all their Love and tenderness. And you possess a heart that has the ability to Love without end, the ability to feel paradise inside yourself as a basic and sincere reaction to yourself and your life, to all that is in existence. There are countless angels, and every speck of matter is full of light, so sit down and realize that you are in the right place. Countless angels see you now, and their Love is not dependent upon anything about you. Their eyes see the depths of you, and they always see beauty, always.

In my opinion, this may be spoken to any being to ever live, even the worst of mankind; there is a freedom within the evolution of energy that we are so that we may follow whatever we desire. Every dark will within man has evolved from the same energy that has produced his most radiant inclinations, and each path will lead to one unifying force; the inevitable completion of a cycle that is the beginning of all evolution, as well as its ending. I believe there are countless angels with their eyes and their hearts quite focused upon all within this world. Of course, this is my opinion which I did not come up with all on my own, but it is what it is, and to me it is beautiful. Ask for Love and healing from angels, and be thankful. They will not force upon you anything you don't ask for.

Years Ago

It was years ago when a fire was ignited. Its fury burned and set me ablaze as a seeker. It was Love that moved me so, and it was the shattering of that Love that unleashed great power within me to seek…the Truth, an experience of the Divine, the reasons why there could be such horrible suffering in myself, and in anyone else. And after so much spiritual seeking, contemplation of depths, and meditation, what I feel I always return to is what we experience in Love; true, deep, profound Love. There could be no meaning to any experience in life and death, and yet, I would still be overcome with the power and beauty of what it means to make Love to one I am completely attracted to, inside and out.

What great purpose, or meaning of life need there be while such beauty exists in living? What else need there be than looking in another's eyes when you are all alone and feeling totally at peace with all that could ever be just because that moment exists and the two of you are so enamored by one another? Yes, there is pain, suffering, severe agony, and much else, and I feel that my life has shown me more of that than any joy or ease of living; but the beauty I feel in it all, even the worst pains, lifts me like on a breeze. There is something gentle in us, in the air, and it may be felt at times. I so deeply wish for all to feel that gentleness, that sense of peace and Love.

The first really clear time I felt it was amidst great pain; mental emotional, spiritual, and physical suffering cut deep, and then, everything in me came to a stop, and the gentle breeze took me in her arms. I felt as if life, or God, or angels had taken me up a bit and held me close to their hearts. There was a silence to all else but the sheer beauty of the miracle that is existence...trees in the wind, birds in the sky, flowers, and colors, and God. I do believe She is real, however different than men have thought Her to be. She is beyond all description, and way beyond male or female. I will never forget that day, I started meditation that day, and it stands in my memory as something rare and remarkable.

Take My Heart

Take my heart to where Lovers kiss and new passions play

To where sorrows miss and naked bodies lay

To the unseen spirit of life

I ask, "Need I any more strife?"

Into my heart you see

So bless it be

And tell it to me

Her name, her hour, and all that Love shall flower

Let our union be one that is truly pure

Let it be one to stop the allure

Of all else for us, and for any near enough to behold

Let us Love as never before told

Let it shine so radiant it blinds the world

And by the beauty of Love may this sphere be hurled

Into days of peace and warm tidings

To more than two show our findings

To all who desire to feel Love

Lift your eyes and just be Loved from above

And you will know what it is to be blessed

Not because you passed God's test

You are worthy of such beauty

Of feeling proud and strong

Of just feeling Love

Let our hearts roar like the loudest thunder

And send every sadness asunder

For our Love be as those flashes of light and wonder

But as one that halts ablaze and lingers for a life

To Not Suffer

If you desire to suffer as little as possible in this life
then simply make enough money to live comfortably
enough with a mate, no kids, maybe some pets, and keep
completely to yourselves as is possible. But make sure
it is not someone you Love very much, or that deeply
Loves you. And make sure that any pets are not those
you grow too attached to. Do not desire much at all. Just
live and go about your routine. Do not exercise, or have
much sex, or drink; and whatever you do don't desire
to grow, to expand, or to experience anything powerful.
Do not seek the truth, or God, or your self because they
will lead you to experiences meant to offer you growth,
and expansion, and power within. Do not seek or desire
anything remarkable, anything of depth, or of any worth
beyond this life because they will show you pain. Do not
desire to laugh all your laughs, because in order to do so
you will be required to cry all your tears, to paraphrase

and twist the words of Khalil Gibran. Just don't make any progress in yourself and you will be safe. But you will also be destined to repeat this level of being over and over again until your consciousness accepts the evolution that beckons all things.

The Beauty

The historical man that existed and whom we call Jesus today is believed to have asked us to Love each other as we Love ourselves. Today we tend to focus upon his message of Loving others, and treating others the way we want to be treated, but I am struck by the presumption he makes within that simple statement; he presumes that we are at least attempting to truly Love our own self. And so, Love your self, whoever you are, no matter what you say, think, feel, do, or look like, and always believe that you are worthy of your own Love and respect. That is the essence of unconditional universal Love, it is no matter what and endless, the beauty of which is truly awe inspiring.

Let all that you are and have been be erased in this moment. You have never done anything wrong. You have never been mistreated, un-liked, or un-Loved. You have never looked in the mirror and disliked what you saw. Now. There is only now, no yesterday. And now you are a beautiful thing in this infinite existence in which there are so many wonderful things that await you to experience. What you are is a free individualized mind, and your mind has the power to create thought, and your thoughts and emotions over time are what shape and color your experience. You are a creator of light and life; Love yourself as this worthy and free creator. You are complete and pure within. So, know that the power is in your mind, to think as you will, and you may take up partnership with your destiny to shape and color more peace, more calm belief in life, and far more beauty than your past has shown you. But the power is in your mind to see, and in the most horribly painful past may be seen peace and purpose. It is my thinking that would say to you that after you choose to take your last breath here you will see that there is great enough purpose in all suffering to give you true peace.

In Times of Pain and Suffering

In times of pain and suffering go back to the basics. Drink lots of water, take a daily multi-vitamin, do plenty of aerobic exercise, exercise your body, and focus on your body in healthy ways. I do not recommend fast food at all, or sodas, or energy drinks; if you don't fill your body with a ton of crap then it will be far easier for you to feel less crappy. Drink orange juice. In times of pain and suffering all that was good in life may seem to come to a stop; we would seek to get things moving in positive ways within you. Take all the quiet time you need or can find, but get moving as well. In times of pain and suffering it is our self-respect, our self-worth, and self-Love that is central to our depression, as well as to our progression from deeply hurt states. So no matter what, I suggest that you believe you are worthy of your own respect, of your own belief in yourself, and in the movement of your powerful and purposeful life. Put forth the effort to do the things you know will make you feel good about yourself, and also the effort not to do the things that will make you feel bad about yourself. Exercise makes us all feel better about ourselves; it releases positive chemicals within your body.

Maybe you are consumed by the thought that another doesn't Love you, but if they ever truly did then I promise you that they do, even if they don't think so. Likewise, if you ever truly Loved them, you always will. If there was ever a deep connection it will always exist in its most essential form. This does not mean that you are meant to be together, or that you should be together, or even that they feel Love in their heart for you right now. Things can get blocked in us, and it is a typical natural defense mechanism for us to block others out of our hearts at times, and what we feel for another is so intimately tied to our own thoughts and feelings about our self. What is truly important is where your power lies, and that is in your beliefs about the situation, about yourself, about your life, and your universe. It will always be within your free power to Love someone who does not seem to Love you anymore. And it is that effort, that warm and benevolent giving of Love that will be one of the most healing things for you, but do not forget to stand strong in your mind and guard your thoughts about yourself. It is beautiful to forgive and give Love to another, but there is not as much sense in doing that if you turn to yourself in only shame and loathing.

In times of pain and suffering you may feel so alone, unworthy, and unloved, and for all those that feel any such way I pray. I pray for you to find healing in every way imaginable, and in all the ways you have yet to imagine possible. In times of pain and suffering listen to yourself. I was always told that I should listen to others, and I used to do that a lot, but the more time has gone on I have come to find through experience that things work out better when I listen to myself more; even if others look at certain situations and see them as mistakes, or failures, they do not see the truth in my opinion. I listen to what others say and I consider their understandings, but I listen to what I think far more now and it has given me a deeper sense of worth and power. But don't simply listen to me.

In times of pain and suffering, or in times of peace and Love listen to your own self because therein lies your divine birthright to be the free and powerful creator of your own self. I hope that you come to believe in times of pain and suffering, in their purpose, in their great value, in their beauty, and in their honor to experience amidst the evolution of a soul's perfect lives. No matter how much pain and suffering you experience here, there will come many times in your soul's experience that you look at yourself and all existence, and send out a joyful thought and feeling that proclaims, "My God…the unspeakable, unappreciable, unknowable, and unbelievable beauty! It is too much, there is so much Love in me and everywhere I see and I am so deeply thankful."

The Great Joy

Life here can be so much different than what we are taught is possible, or probable. In my opinion, we have not had a clear understanding of life at all; and with a better understanding the game changes completely from what has been, in general, throughout all of human history. It is like we have been playing baseball by the rules of soccer. A few slight changes in our understanding of some fundamental rules may revolutionize our experience. We have been seeing pain, suffering, and death so negatively. We have not appreciated or accepted en masse that we create our own experience with our thoughts, emotions, words, and actions. We are taught that things in life happen to us, not through us. The universe, all of creation, and every living being is laughably diminished every day within every classroom and every mind that thinks a thought. This is the case simply because it is all so much better than we have previously thought. Yes, this is dramatic and stuff but whatever man, we are all worth much more than we know, it is all far less serious than we know, and it can all get a lot better than you know.

If you would begin to exercise some deliberate filtering of negative thoughts and emotions to focus on more and more positivity you would begin to be happier. And the happier you become the more happiness you will attract into your life. But you have the Source within you, you are the creator, and you may focus on what you will. You may raise your vibration by focusing upon freedom, abundance, harmony, unconditional self-worth, unconditional Love, beauty, power, trust, and great joy; or you may seemingly enslave yourself within your own creation of misery, lack of worth, fear, and powerlessness. The only thing standing between you and great joy is your own choices of thought, feeling, and perception because these things are the most important game changers. Your thoughts and your emotions create manifestation of things at like vibrational levels. Fearful thoughts practiced with enough consistency will create negative emotions, and eventually negative experiences in life. Life is a dynamic mirror; if you learn to truly and consistently smile into the mirror, then you will see a smile in the reflection, in the manifestations of emotion, experience, and event.

In my opinion, these lives on this planet are a beautiful system set up by our own brilliant, joyous, and powerful free choice so that our experience will expand, so that fun will continue, so that we may find ourselves seeking and achieving dreams to the point of self- dissolution into pure orgasmic completion. This may seem far from the reality of so much human life, but I slyly smile and wink and humbly suggest that there is so much more going on than you or I know; and it ain't bad, it ain't a fucking tragedy, not you or anyone is ever truly weak or worthless, and all occurs with great power, with great purpose, intention, freedom, beauty, and desire for more…more, more! More!…endless expansion, infinite velocity, endless fun, infinite sexiness, endless amazement, infinite Love, and musical rapture, and knowing, and blossoming of dreams…the Fates, the Power, and the Great Joy.